Spy Kid

REAL SPY GADGETS

Deanna Caswell

BLACK
RABBIT
BOOKS

Hi Jinx is published by Black Rabbit Books
P.O. Box 3263, Mankato, Minnesota, 56002.
www.blackrabbitbooks.com
Copyright © 2019 Black Rabbit Books

Marysa Storm, editor; Michael Sellner, designer;
Grant Gould, production designer;
Omay Ayres, photo researcher

Library of Congress Cataloging-in-Publication Data
Names: Caswell, Deanna, author.
Title: Real spy gadgets / by Deanna Caswell.
Description: Mankato, Minnesota : Black Rabbit Books,
2019. | Series: Hi Jinx. Spy Kid | Includes bibliographical
references and index.
Identifiers: LCCN 2017053752 (print) | LCCN 2018012082
(ebook) | ISBN 9781680725964 (e-book) | ISBN
9781680725902 (library binding) | ISBN 9781680727449
(paperback)
Subjects: LCSH: Espionage–Equipment and supplies–Juvenile
literature. | Electronic surveillance–Juvenile literature. |
Espionage–Juvenile literature. | Spies–Juvenile literature.
Classification: LCC UB270.5 (ebook) | LCC UB270.5 .C387 2019
(print) | DDC 327.12028/4–dc23
LC record available at https://lccn.loc.gov/2017053752

Printed in the United States. 4/18

Image Credits

commons.wikimedia.org: Shaun Verssy, 12 (shoe, tree);
WolfenSilva, 10 (pen); dealsonly.com: Covert Coins, 10–11 (coin);
discountsbargain.com: AARON DEVIS, 8 (camera); Getty: AFP, 8
(photo in glass); Bettmann, 8 (photo); iStock: Agustinc, Cover (spy,
city bkgd), 2–3, 4 (city bkgd, spy), 14, 18 (spy), 20 (hand), 23 (spy);
CSA Images/ B&W Mex Ink Collection, 4 (bttm); Thodoris_Tibilis,
Cover (glass), 8 (glass), 21 (glass); Shutterstock: Alexandr III, 3;
amesto, 16 (man); Auspicious, 10 (rat); Bankrx, 7; DinoZ, 20
(top secret); Dn Br, 16 (flashlight); Dream Master, 19 (compass);
eelnosiva, 12 (poo); Gorodenkoff, 6–7; grynold, 4 (people in
park); Igor Zakowski, 10 (brick); inklisem, Cover (starry bkgd);
kstudija, 4 (trees); LAUDiseno, 1, 18–19 (glass); Lemonade
Serenade, Cover (bttm); nikiteev_konstantin, 4 (pen), 10 (note);
NikomMaelao Production, Cover (moon); opicobello, 17 (torn
paper); Pasko Maksim, Back Cover (top), 9 (bttm), 17 (bttm), 23
(top), 24; phipatbig, 4 (hand); Pitju, 18 (page curl), 21 (page curl);
Ron Dale, 5, 9 (top); RTRO, 15; totallypic, 8 (arrow) Every effort has
been made to contact copyright holders for material reproduced in
this book. Any omissions will be rectified in subsequent printings if
notice is given to
the publisher.

CONTENTS

Chapter 1
SPY GEAR

The agent unscrews his pen. Out drops a **microdot**. The microdot is small. But it holds big enemy plans. The spy puts the microdot in a hollow coin. He then walks into a park. As the spy passes a bench, he drops the coin. He can only hope his contact picks it up in time.

Top Secret

Spies watch and listen for their governments. They collect information about enemies and other governments. Spies' jobs are often difficult. They need the right tools to get them done. Many spy tools are **classified**. Here are some spy gadgets the public knows about.

Chapter 2
REAL SPY GADGETS

Spies often use cameras to gather secrets. After all, a picture is worth 1,000 words.

During the **Cold War**, **Soviet Union** spies used cameras hidden in their coats. A button was actually a tiny camera. To snap pictures, a spy simply squeezed a cable in the coat pocket.

Spies also put cameras in pens. Some watches could take pictures too.

Spies once put small cameras on pigeons.

Get the Message Out

Spies use gear to pass messages too. Their pens, screws, and coins had secret compartments for notes. Spies have also used fake rocks and bricks to store information. Some spies even left notes in dead rats! These items look normal. No one suspects they carry important information.

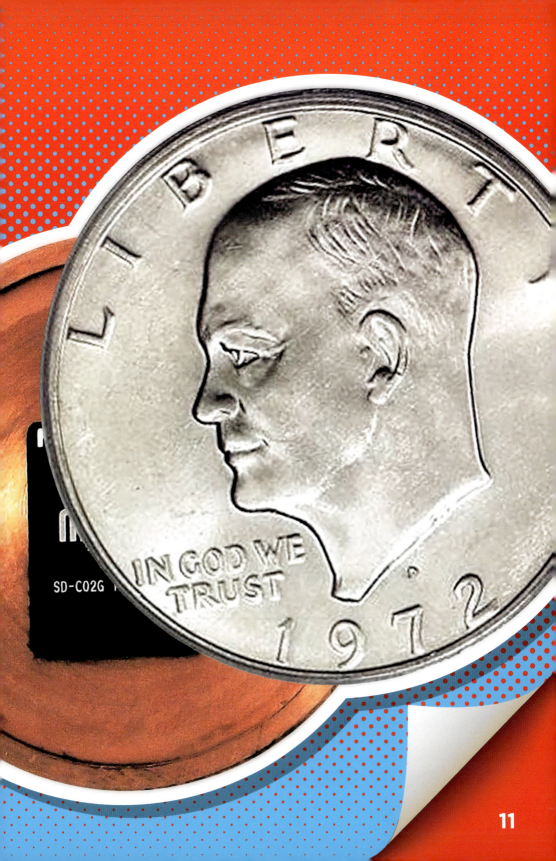

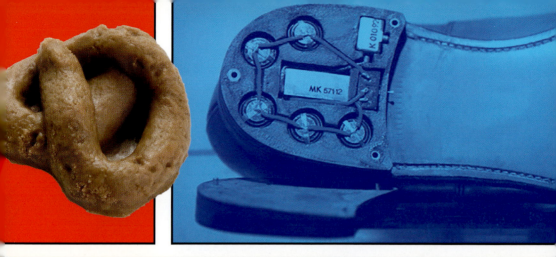

The CIA once turned a cat into a spy.
The cat had a microphone in its ear. It had
a **transmitter** near its skull. People took the cat
to a park to test it. Unfortunately, the cat
walked into a nearby street. A car hit and killed it.

Communicate!

Spies use gear to listen in on conversations. Tiny recorders and transmitters can hide nearly anywhere.

Is that a tree stump? No, it's a **solar**-powered transmitter! During the 1970s, spies placed a fake tree stump outside **Moscow**. A transmitter in the stump **intercepted** messages from an air base.

Spies also hid transmitters in the heels of shoes. They used fake poop too. That's right! Spies used fake dog poop transmitters in the 1970s.

Sabotage

Spies often ruin enemy plans. Sometimes they do it with a bang. Spies have blown up bridges and buildings to slow down enemies. Their explosives had to look like normal items, though.

Some spies used bombs painted to look like lumps of coal. They'd leave them in coal piles. When people threw the coal-bombs into fire, they would explode.

15

Weapons

Most spies do their best to avoid fighting. But sometimes they have no choice. Just like their cameras, their weapons are hidden. Guns may look like flashlights or pipes. Even a lipstick tube can be a gun.

Pens or umbrellas may shoot poison pellets or hide needles.

Finding Their Way

Spies' jobs usually take them to **foreign** lands. They need maps and compasses to find their ways. Spies have hidden tiny compasses in plain sight. Many compasses could be found in buttons. Maps can be harder to hide. One spy used playing cards. Removing the cards' top layers revealed map sections.

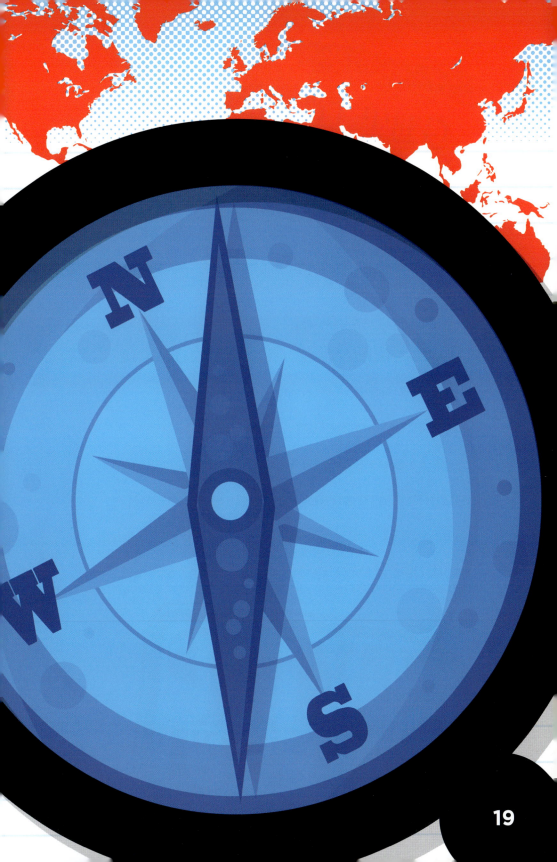

Chapter 3
GET IN ON THE HI JINX

Spies use a lot of the same gear they did many years ago. Spy technology is always improving, though. Listening devices have gotten smaller and stronger. Someday, the CIA might use TVs to spy on people. Real insects might carry small recorders too. But we won't really know what future spies will use. Their gear will be top secret.

Take It One Step More

1. How are real spy gadgets similar to those used in movies? How are they different?

2. Spy gear often looks like everyday items. Make a list of five objects you use every day. How could they be used to spy?

3. If you were a spy, what supplies would you take on a mission?

GLOSSARY

classified (KLAS-uh-fahyd)—kept secret from all but a few people in the government

Cold War (KOHLD WAWR)—the nonviolent conflict between the United States and Soviet Union that lasted from 1945 to 1991

foreign (FAWR-in)—in a place or country other than the one a person is from

intercept (in-tur-SEPT)—to secretly receive a communication or signal directed somewhere else

microdot (MAHY-kro-dot)—a photographic reproduction of printed matter reduced to the size of a dot; people use special magnifying viewers to read microdots.

Moscow (MOS-koh)—the capital city of Russia; Moscow was the capital of the Soviet Union.

solar (SO-lur)—relating to the sun

Soviet Union (SOH-ve-uht YOON-yun)—a former country in eastern Europe and northern Asia

transmitter (tranz-MIH-tuhr)—a device that sends out radio or TV signals

BOOKS

Caswell, Deanna. *Famous Spy Missions.* Spy Kid. Mankato, MN: Black Rabbit Books, 2019.

Kallen, Stuart A. *World War II Spies and Secret Agents.* Heroes of World War II. Minneapolis: Lerner Publications, 2018.

Larson, Kirsten W. *The CIA.* Protecting Our People. Mankato, MN: Amicus High Interest, 2017.

WEBSITES

FBI — Kids
archives.fbi.gov/archives/fun-games/kids

KidSpy Zone
www.spymuseum.org/education-programs/kids-families/kidspy-zone/

Kids' Zone
https://www.cia.gov/kids-page

INDEX